Lizards

Laura Marsh

NATIONAL
GEOGRAPHIC

Washington, D.C.

For Andie and Jed
—L. F. M.

Paperback ISBN: 978-1-4263-0922-9   Library ISBN: 978-1-4263-0923-6

Photo credits

Cover, Kim Taylor/npl/Minden Pictures; 1, Martin Harvey/Corbis; 2, Flickr RF/Getty Images; 4-5, Theo Allofs/Corbis; 6 (top), blickwinkel/Alamy; 6-7, Levent Songur/iStockphoto; 7 (top), fivespots/Shutterstock; 7 (center), Eric Isselée/Shutterstock; 8, Jeff Ross/National Geographic My Shot; 9 (top), Conrad Maufe/naturepl.com; 9 (bottom), Ray Bird/Frank Lane Picture Agency/Corbis; 10-11, Lauren Hogan/National Geographic My Shot; 12 (top), Tim Laman/ National Geographic Stock; 12 (bottom), Visuals Unlimited/Getty Images; 12-13 (background), Jack Hollingsworth/Photodisc/Getty Images; 13 (top), Ocean/Corbis; 13 (bottom), Peter Scoones/naturepl.com; 14 (top), Robert Valentic/naturepl.com/; 14 (bottom), Tom Walker/Riser/Getty Images; 15, Cathy Keifer/iStockphoto; 16-17, Photo Researchers RM/Getty Images; 18, Wild Wonders of Europe/Lesniewski/naturepl.com/; 19, Kim Murrell/Shutterstock; 20, Chris Johns/National Geographic Stock; 21, Nick Garbutt/naturepl.com; 22, Udaya Wijesoma/National Geographic My Shot; 23, Inaki Relanzon/naturepl.com; 24 (top), John Cancalosi/Alamy; 24 (bottom), Tim Flach/Stone/Getty Images; 24-25 (background), Jack Hollingsworth/Photodisc/Getty Images; 25 (top), imagebroker/Alamy; 25 (bottom), Animals Animals/SuperStock; 26, WaterFrame RM/Getty Images; 27, Juniors Bildarchiv; 28 (top left), fivespots/Shutterstock; 28 (top right), Pan Xunbin/Shutterstock; 28 (bottom left), Eric Isselée/Shutterstock; 28 (bottom right), fivespots/Shutterstock; 29, Nicolette Raley/ National Geographic Your Shot; 30 (left), Sebastian Duda/Shutterstock; 30 (right), Eric Isselée/Shutterstock; 30-31 (background) Jack Hollingsworth/Photodisc/Getty Images; 31 (top left), Michal Filip Gmerek/Shutterstock; 31 (top right), Darlyne A. Murawski/National Geographic Stock; 31 (bottom left), Patrick Rolands/Shutterstock; 31 (bottom right), Cathy Keifer/Shutterstock; 32 (top left), Nick Garbutt/naturepl.com; 32 (top right), Curtis Kautzer/Shutterstock; 32 (center left), WaterFrame RM/Getty Images; 32 (center right), Peter Betts/Shutterstock; 32 (bottom left), Tim Flach/Stone/Getty Images; 32 (bottom right), Lauren Hogan/National Geographic My Shot.

Printed in the United States of America

13/WOR/2

Table of Contents

What am I?

I can be as big as a table.
I can be as small as a pin.
I can swim, glide, or run.

My skin is smooth,
bumpy, or even
thorny.

Thorny devil

What am I?

A lizard!

Reptiles

Baja blue rock lizard

Lizards come in different colors. They come in different shapes.

But all lizards are reptiles. A reptile has dry skin with scales. It usually lays eggs on land. It has a backbone.

Nile crocodile

Turtles, snakes, crocodiles, and tortoises are also reptiles.

Leopard tortoise

Corn snake

Tail Term

SCALES:
Small, hard
plates that
cover the skin

A reptile doesn't make its own body heat. To warm up, it lies in the sun. To cool down, it lies in the shade.

Iguana

Most lizards live in warm places.
They live in the desert and by the sea.
They live in forests and mountains.
Lizards live on every continent
except Antarctica.

Monitor

Scaly Skin

Jackson's chameleon

Lizard skin can be smooth and shiny. It can be bumpy or spiky. But every lizard has tiny scales.

Scales protect lizards. They keep a lizard's body from getting hurt. They keep a lizard warm. Scales keep a lizard from losing water, too.

11

Super Lizards

It's a bird, it's a plane, it's . . . a lizard?
Check out these lizard superpowers:

Draco lizard

The Draco lizard is also called the "flying dragon." You can see why. It glides through the air. Its folds of skin look like wings.

Basilisk lizard

This lizard runs on water! And it's fast, too. Its long back toes keep it from sinking.

Say *BASS-i-lisk*

Gecko lizard

The gecko lizard can walk on walls and ceilings. Special hairs on its feet make it stick to surfaces.

Marine iguana

This lizard is a great swimmer. Its powerful tail helps it swim and dive.

Say *ih-GWA-nuh*

Mealtime

Most lizards are meat-eaters. They snack on bugs. They eat small animals.

Some are plant-eaters. They munch on flowers. They also eat fruits and leaves.

Knob-tailed gecko

Santa Fe land iguana

Chameleon

This chameleon has a long, sticky tongue. It shoots out in a flash! The tongue grabs a bug. Mmmm, yum. It's dinnertime!

Babies

Almost all lizards hatch from eggs. Only a few lizards are born live.

A mother lizard lays her eggs. Then she leaves. Most lizard parents don't take care of their young. Baby lizards can take care of themselves.

Iguana

Legless Lizards

Did you know . . . some lizards don't have legs? Legless lizards look like snakes. You have to look closely to tell them apart.

European legless lizard

eyelid

ear hole

But legless lizards have eyelids that move. They also have ear holes. Snakes don't have these.

Rough green snake

no eyelid

no ear hole on the outside

Hide and Seek

Can you find the lizards?

Lizards are good at hiding. They can look like trees, leaves, flowers, and rocks. They can look like moss and sand, too.

Jackson's chameleon

Camouflage keeps lizards safe. Predators can't see them.

Say CAM-oh-flahj

Tail Term

CAMOUFLAGE: An animal's natural color or shape that helps hide it from an enemy

Tail Term

PREDATOR: An animal that eats other animals

Leaf-tailed gecko

Look at Me!

But lizards don't always hide. Lizards like to show off, too. They want to get noticed by a mate.

Common forest lizard

Tail Term

MATE: A partner to have babies with

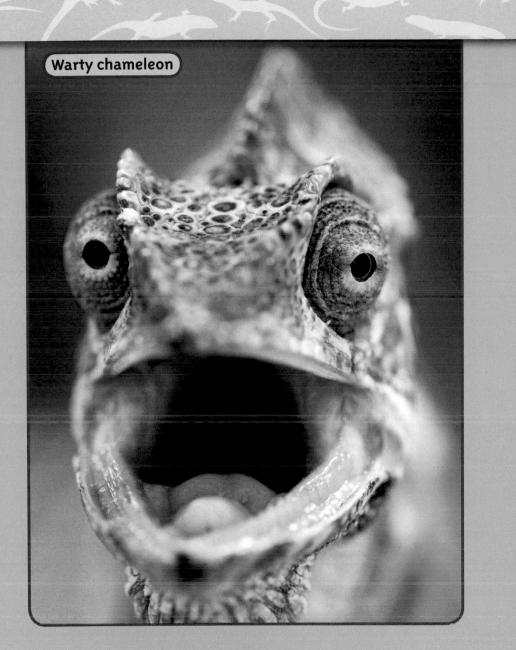

Warty chameleon

Some proudly show their colorful skin. Some sing. And some lizards just try to look big and strong.

Great Escapes

These lizards scare off their enemies.
Then they make a quick getaway.

Nasty trick

The horned toad lizard shoots blood from its eyes! But the lizard is not hurt. It's just a trick.

Bad bite

The gila monster is a poisonous lizard. Its bite is painful. It can make other animals sick.

Say *HEE-la*

Scary costume

The frilled lizard puffs out its collar. It stands on its back legs. It hisses loudly. And it runs fast!

Losing a tail

An animal bites a gecko's tail. The tail falls off! The enemy watches it twitch on the ground. The lizard escapes. A new tail will grow back in its place.

Tail Term

POISONOUS: Something that can cause hurt, illness, or death

Biggest and Smallest

The biggest lizard is the Komodo dragon. An adult is longer than a picnic table!

Komodo dragons can grow to ten feet long.

It has sharp claws and teeth. It eats large prey like water buffalo. It sometimes eats other Komodo dragons.

The smallest lizard is the dwarf gecko. It's a little more than a half-inch long. That's about the size of a pushpin.

ACTUAL
SIZE

William's dwarf gecko

Lots of Lizards

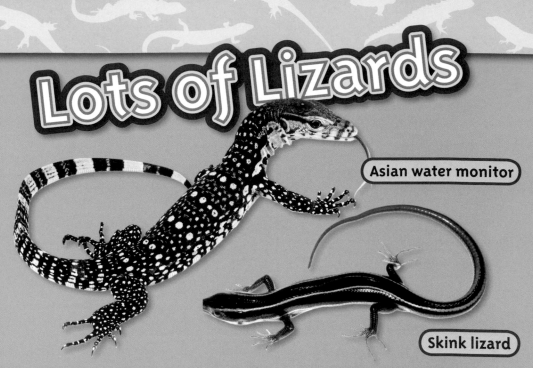

Asian water monitor

Skink lizard

There are more than 3,000 kinds of lizards on Earth. They are each special in their own way.

Let's hear it for lizards!

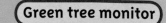

Green tree monitor

Leopard gecko

Q What do you call a lizard wearing earplugs?

A Anything you like. It can't hear you!

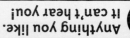

What in the World?

These pictures show close-up views of lizardy things. Use the hints below to figure out what's in the pictures. Answers on page 31.

1

HINT: This can grip a rock or branch easily.

2

HINT: These protect lizards in many ways.

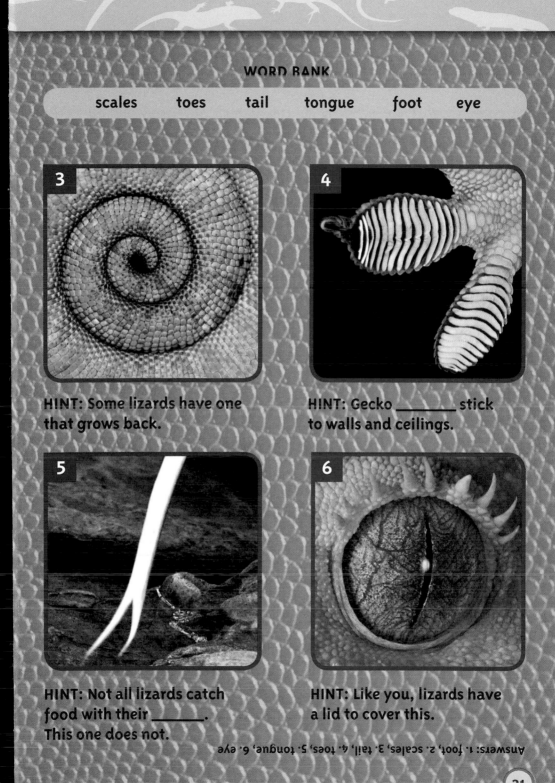

WORD BANK

| scales | toes | tail | tongue | foot | eye |

3

HINT: Some lizards have one that grows back.

4

HINT: Gecko _____ stick to walls and ceilings.

5

HINT: Not all lizards catch food with their _____. This one does not.

6

HINT: Like you, lizards have a lid to cover this.

Answers: 1. foot, 2. scales, 3. tail, 4. toes, 5. tongue, 6. eye

CAMOUFLAGE: An animal's natural color or shape that helps hide it from an enemy

MATE: A partner to have babies with

PREDATOR: An animal that eats other animals

PREY: An animal that is eaten by another animal

POISONOUS: Something that can cause hurt, illness, or death

SCALES: Small hard plates that cover the skin